Graphic conception:
Sandra Brys

translation: Brian Sullivan of the Alliance
Française of Boston and Cambridge

© Casterman, Tournai 1994
Published by
Charlesbridge Publishing
85 Main Street, Watertown, MA 02172
(617) 926-0329
All rights reserved, including the
right of reproduction in whole or in
part in any form. Printed in Belgium.
10 9 8 7 6 5 4 3 2 1

Library of Congress Cataloging-in-Publication Data
Sart, Jean de.
    [Animaux qui font peur.   English]
    Scary animals / by Jean de Sart; illustrated by
Jean-Marie Winants.
        p.   cm.
    ISBN 0-88106-694-X (library reinforced)
    ISBN 0-88106-674-5 (trade hardcover)
    1. Animals—Juvenile literature. 2. Dangerous
animals—Juvenile literature. [1. Animals.
2. Dangerous animals.]   I. Winants, Jean-Marie, ill.
II. Title.
QL49.S1713   1994
591—dc20   93-20963
                                                          CIP
                                                          AC

SCARY ANIMALS

by Jean de Sart

illustrated by Jean-Marie Winants

Charlesbridge

A vulture, wolf, or snake may scare you, but each obeys the same fundamental laws that all other animals do, to survive and to perpetuate their species. To get what they need, and to overcome difficulties, they use their instinct. This includes behaviors that are inborn and also the capacity to learn by watching other members of their species.

A scary animal may have an important role in the balance of nature. Snakes and bats have as much a right to live as the more appealing kittens or butterflies. If we can forget our largely unjustified fears and leave our squeamishness behind, we can learn the truth about the animals that scare us. More acceptance of these animals will help us see that the natural world fits together like a puzzle. Each of its parts is indispensable for its beauty, elegance, and balance.

Danger

Real, exaggerated, or imaginary danger is the reason that is most often used to justify fear. We know that the wasp's sting is painful, that certain snakes are venomous, and that some predators attack people. Often, however, our fear and ignorance of animal behavior leads us to exaggerate the danger. Our fear turns into panic, increasing the risk rather than diminishing it. Other reasons contribute to our mistrust or fear of some animals. Let's investigate some of these reasons.

Slithering

The movement of slithering animals usually worries us. This method of moving, often hidden at ground level, arouses our fear almost automatically. In addition, we tend to think that slithering is a trait of "inferior" or evil animals.

In order to change our attitudes and our behaviors toward wildlife, it is a good idea to begin by questioning our fears. We do not always know why a particular animal seems scary. Our responses toward an animal depend on the teaching of our culture, traditions, and the historical period. For example, one type of poisonous snake was considered a god by ancient Egyptians who praised it, while other cultures feared it.

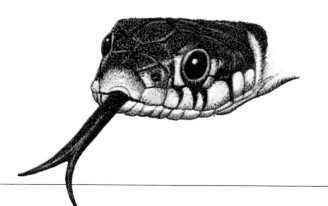

Eyes

People express much of their feelings through their facial expressions. Certain animals have a fixed stare due to the absence of moving eyelids. Creatures that hunt often have a very intense stare. This stare is sometimes associated with "ferocity," because people tend to apply human intentions or feelings to these animals.

Hunting

People who eat meat are carnivorous predators. We find this perfectly normal. We equally accept animal predators that do not offend our sensitivities. The ladybug devouring hundreds of aphids does not upset us because we find the ladybug pretty and the aphids destructive. But when the predator draws blood from its victims, especially from those that belong to well known "likable" species, it is upsetting. Thus, we cannot easily accept a fox eating a vole or a lynx eating a rabbit.

Beliefs / Superstitions

Beliefs are the most mysterious basis for human reactions towards animals. Since a very long time ago, people have asked themselves questions about the nature of good and evil. People have also identified their anguishes, worries, and fears with animals. Certain animals became associated with qualities such as craftiness, patience, wickedness, cruelty, gentleness, and so on. These qualities vary greatly sometimes from one country or tradition to another, but this imagery has often prevented the objective analysis of animal behavior.

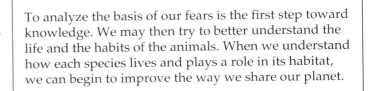

To analyze the basis of our fears is the first step toward knowledge. We may then try to better understand the life and the habits of the animals. When we understand how each species lives and plays a role in its habitat, we can begin to improve the way we share our planet.

THE GARDEN SPIDER

In May, a few days after leaving its cocoon, the garden spider, also known as the cross-bearing spider, begins to look around. Without being taught, it knows what to do. First it climbs the dry stem of a carrot-like plant until it reaches the top. From its lookout, the spider observes the garden. A light breeze ruffles the blades of grass.

The spider is aware of the direction of the wind. It unwinds a string of silk that the breeze carries across the pale, purple wild flowers. Success! One end of the silk string is now attached to the plant where the spider stands, and the other end is attached to a plant about a foot away. With the first cable cast, the careful work begins.

Patiently, the spider weaves and winds the silk with the accuracy of an architect. Finally, the skillful work is completed. The spider hides behind a nearby leaf to wait. It is still attached to the net by one thread.

The spider does not have to wait long. The net shakes and pulls as a tiny, two-winged fly struggles in the sticky lines.

The spider is ready. It neatly wraps its silk around the fly so that it cannot move and then bites, killing the prey with its venom. The spider drinks the juices from the body of the fly. A fine meal!

As night approaches, the prey becomes more abundant. No longer hungry, the spider stores its victims in woven cases of threads and attaches them to the web where they were caught. The first week in the life of the garden spider has not gone badly. It was able to satisfy its hunger and store food for later. All would be wonderful except that a little brown bird, a wren, is searching among the shrubs and low bushes. It is very fond of eating spiders!

LOCATION	DESCRIPTION	HABITAT	BEHAVIOR

LOCATION

• The garden spider is widespread throughout the Northern Hemisphere.

DESCRIPTION

• The garden spider is brownish yellow and black. The female garden spider has a white cross on its abdomen.
• The garden spider has a small head and eight small bulging eyes.
• Four pairs of legs, made up of 7 segments each, carry its light body.
• In the front of its head, the garden spider has 2 arm-like extensions that are used for eating.
• The body has three parts: head, thorax (chest), and abdomen (stomach).
• The male is generally only half the size of the female. The male is $1/8$ to $1/4$ inch and the female is $3/8$ to $1/2$ inch.

HABITAT

♀

• The garden spider lives in orchards, hedges, gardens, bushes, and brush.

BEHAVIOR

• In its body, the spider has six pairs of glands that make silk for webs. The garden spider makes a web that resembles a wheel. The threads of the outer and inner circles and the lines that radiate like the spokes of the wheel are not sticky. The spider uses these to move along the web. The threads of the inner concentric circles are sticky. At times the spider will cling to the center point of the web, but it usually hides on a leaf near the web where it is connected by a thread so that it can feel when prey has been caught.

10

FOOD

• The garden spider eats small insects.

REPRODUCTION

• The garden spider is an adult by autumn. After the female mates and eats her male partner, she lays several hundred yellow eggs in a safe spot underneath the bark of a tree. The female will die during the first frosts of winter, but her eggs will hatch the next spring if they survive the cold.

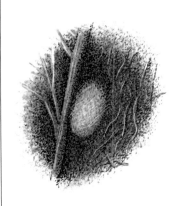

THE GARDEN SPIDER AND PEOPLE

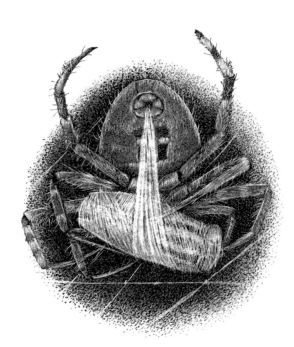

• Spiders make humans even more nervous than the six-legged insects. People fear the thought of eight little legs crawling on their skin! In addition, the sudden movements that spiders can make after being still for so long frighten the everyday observer. The white cross on the female's back also makes humans think that the spider is marked for a reason—Beware! Stay back! Nevertheless, of about 35,000 species of spiders, only 10 or so are dangerous to people.

THREATS

• Garden spiders have numerous predators: birds, lizards, frogs, toads, certain insects, and small mammals. Even spiders themselves have been known to eat each other. These predatory actions are all part of the food chain. It is not for food that humans kill spiders. It is out of fear. We also indirectly kill spiders when we destroy places where they like to live by pulling out weeds and trimming hedges and bushes around our homes and public buildings.

THE BAT

A colony of bats has chosen the attic of a country farm house to be their home. As night approaches, the people in the house hear small noises, which signal the awakening of the colony. The bats stretch out their long arms and blink their bright eyes. Some yawn widely, revealing a pinkish tongue and small, white, pointy teeth.

One after the other, the small flying mammals come out of hiding. The majority of the females leave to hunt, but a few members of the colony stay behind to nurse the young. The males live alone, apart from these nurseries. They only visit to drop off food to the young or to escort the females home after a night of hunting. When hunting, each bat follows the same flying pattern and seldom alters its course.

One bat is flying near the farmhouse. It flies regularly around the same tree and then at exactly the same spot, will suddenly surge up and circle the building. Sometimes it will perform a rapid turn in the air to snatch a whirling insect.

The bats are very watchful and alert — rarely does an insect escape their notice. Thoroughly absorbed in their hunt, they do not notice a large, whitish bird perched in a pine tree. It is a barn owl that also has young to feed and does not often pass up the chance to catch a bat.

LOCATION	DESCRIPTION	HABITAT	BEHAVIOR	FOOD

• Several species of bats exist in North America, South America, Europe, Asia, Africa, and Australia.
• The common brown (myotis) bat lives almost everywhere in the United States and Canada, with the exception of extreme northern and southern borders.

• The little brown myotis weighs only $1/4$ to $1/3$ ounce and has a wingspan of 6 to 8 inches.
• Bats are the only mammals that really fly. Their hands have evolved into wings with skin stretched between the finger bones and between the arm, the side of the body, and the hind leg.

• Bats are found in all environments. They live near houses and in the open countryside. They can live comfortably in holes of trees, crevices in rocks, or in caves.

• Rarely seen in the daylight, most American species of bats are nocturnal. They fly between 5 and 60 feet off the ground and often follow the same flight path. Bat flight can also be characterized by variations in speed. Although some bats migrate hundreds of miles, others hibernate during the winter.

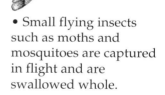

• Small flying insects such as moths and mosquitoes are captured in flight and are swallowed whole.

• Most bats have skin connecting the hind legs and tail.
• Different families of bats include leafnose bats, plainnose bats, vampire bats, and freetail bats. The largest family of bats is the plainnose bat.

REPRODUCTION

• Mating takes place at the end of the summer and sometimes during the winter. Each year, the female gives birth to one or two young.

• The newborn weighs about half an ounce (1.5 grams). Babies may hold onto the mother while she hunts or may be left in a roost in the care of another female bat. They reach full size at the age of 4 weeks.

HUNTING

• In flight, bats make sounds almost constantly. These cries are ultrasonic. People cannot hear them. The sounds go through the air, bounce off insects, and return to the bat. The bat then knows exactly where the prey is. This system allows the bat to hunt without being seen and to determine the size, direction, and speed of its prey.

BATS AND PEOPLE

• Many people are frightened of animals that come out only at night. Superstitions about bats have developed over the years. It was once thought that bats were the companions of witches and werewolves. In many books and movies, bats are associated with vampires, like Dracula. In reality, only three species of bats (which live only in Central and South America) drink the blood of cattle. Most bats eat fruit or insects and are not at all harmful to humans. In fact, bats are very helpful to us because they eat thousands of the bugs that we consider pests.

THREATS AND
MEASURES OF CONSERVATION

• Bats are becoming more and more threatened. The bat needs a varied supply of insects to eat, but we spray our farms and yards with toxic chemicals to kill the very bugs that the bats need. Their food supply is becoming limited in some areas.

SOLUTIONS

• We need to preserve and protect the trees and caves where bats like to live.
• We can also try to limit the use of toxic sprays.

THE WILD BOAR

The wild boars come noisily down through the valley. Upstream from a pond, in a calm branch of the stream, six boars splash and play in the clay-like mud. They roll around, pushing each other from time to time and making short, satisfied snorts.

Their play soon comes to an end. The boars raise their heads, and their eyes become watchful. In the distance, the barking of dogs has invaded their harmony. A male boar sits up and snorts. His powerful chest is sturdy and wide. There is nothing clumsy about this animal. His shoulders and rump are muscled and strong. The snout at the end of the muzzle is large and leathery. He points his hairy ears toward the danger that he senses. His nostrils tremble while his cord-like tail flips up and down to signal approaching danger.

All of the boars pull themselves out of the muddy water. They gallop off in single-file to seek safety in a grove of trees. All, except for one. Angered, the largest male boar decides to fight. From the other side of the pond, a dog appears. The dog's howl sounds out like a trumpet. The stiff hairs on the boar's back stand on end. His jaw tightens and his eyes focus on the dog who is running around the pond coming toward him. The dog stops abruptly face-to-face with the boar and then quickly lunges at him, trying to bite the boar's rear leg. The wild boar is able to gracefully dodge the dog and knock it down.

The wild boar snorts in anger and throws his 300 pounds onto his panting enemy. Wait! Now the wild boar senses another danger close by: the distinctive smell of a human being. The boar knows that he has little chance of defeating this two-legged creature that carries a rifle. Only last year the boar felt the sharp pain of a bullet scraping across his back. The large male decides to escape by heading into the dense underbrush.

LOCATION

- The wild boar is found in many areas of Europe, with the exception of Scandinavia and the British Isles. It has also been introduced into forested parts of the southeastern United States.

DESCRIPTION

- The wild boar is massive in size.
- Generally grayish brown, its coat consists of thick, short bristles. At each site of the snout, a large canine tooth curls up to form a tusk.
- Its length from head to tail is 44 to 55 inches. The tail measures 6 to 8 inches.
- The boar is approximately 35 inches high from the ground to the shoulder.
- The male boar weighs from 132 to 400 pounds, and the female weighs from 77 to 135 pounds.

HABITAT

- The wild boar lives in leafy forests and low, thick bushes. It prefers damp areas and is often close to farmland.

BEHAVIOR

- Especially active at dusk and dawn, the boar rests during the heat of the day. Boars enjoy playing in cool soil and damp mud.
- Quick and agile in times of necessity, the wild boar often changes habitat and can travel long distances.
- The females live in groups with their young. When traveling, an older female generally leads the group. The young follow her, while the other females bring up the rear.

FOOD

• In general, wild boars eat green leafy plants, acorns, beechnuts, and various roots. On occasion, they may also eat rodents, young rabbits, worms, snails, and the eggs of ground-nesting birds. In grassy areas, boars uproot grass in search of worms. On farmland, they also eat grain, potatoes, beets, and grapes.

REPRODUCTION

• Mating takes place in late fall or early winter. The female boar carries the young for four months before they are born in the spring. The litter typically has as many as 10 baby boars. A baby wild boar has a distinct coat of red, brown, and white stripes that go from head to tail.

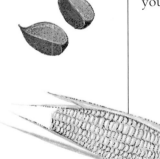

THE WILD BOAR AND PEOPLE

• For centuries, people have hunted the wild boar for sport. Although the wild boar has learned to fear people and to avoid contact with them, it becomes fierce and aggressive if it is wounded, feels cornered, or feels as though its young may be harmed.

This very courage is why people have hunted the boar for sport. It is a challenge to capture and kill such a clever, strong animal.
• People complain when boars damage farmland by eating crops.

THREATS AND MEASURES OF CONSERVATION

• The attitude of many people has been that wild boars exist only to be hunted. People have fenced in the areas where wild boars live so that it is easier to hunt them. The number of boars that live within the fence soon increase as they follow their normal mating habits. Soon, food becomes sparse. The forest is harmed in the area where the boars are trapped because they have no choice but to dig up plants to eat the roots. Eventually, their numbers decrease as their food supplies dwindle.

SOLUTIONS

• Wild boars hunting could be regulated more carefully.
• Fencing wild boars could be banned.

THE COMMON WASP

It has been a long winter, but spring has finally come. Little by little, the temperature becomes milder. A wasp exits from its hide-out where it has slept all winter. It basks in the sun. This is a young queen born at the end of last summer. She had mated just before she hibernated. She rubs her head using her forelegs, vibrates her wings, and suddenly flies away. She is looking for a place to lay her eggs where she can begin a new colony. After visiting and inspecting several shallow spots in the lawn, she chooses a deserted mouse hole in the field.

All alone, the young queen busily starts gathering materials for the construction of a nest. She examines a fence post and begins scraping out rotted wood with the help of her strong jaws. She removes fine shavings and dampens them with her saliva. The shavings become a sort of paper pulp which she first uses to build a small, hollow ball the size of a walnut. Next, on the inside of this ball, she prepares 10 to 20 cells in a honeycomb pattern. In each cell, the queen lays an egg. Very quickly, larvae hatch.

The queen takes care of them, feeding them finely ground flies and caterpillars. A few weeks later, the larvae undergo a great change and become adult wasps. These first offspring are all workers who will help enlarge the wasps' nest. They will also hunt for food and feed new larvae that hatch. From now until the end of summer, the queen's only job is to lay as many eggs as she can.

LOCATION	DESCRIPTION	HABITAT	BEHAVIOR

Queen   Worker   Male

LOCATION

• The common wasp lives in all of Europe, North and Central America, Australia, and Asia.

Bee — note how body segments are connected

DESCRIPTION

• Body length varies among members of the colony. The workers are about half an inch long, and the males are less than half an inch. The queens are just over an inch.
• The body is black with yellow stripes.
• Two pairs of wings fold back along the length of the body when it is at rest.
• The wings consist of a clear, thin membrane. The body is composed of three parts: the head, the thorax (chest), and the abdomen (stomach). The link between the thorax and abdomen is very thin.

HABITAT

• The common wasp is easily observed because it lives in many habitats: city parks, gardens, fields, and forests. It is often found close to a source of water.

BEHAVIOR

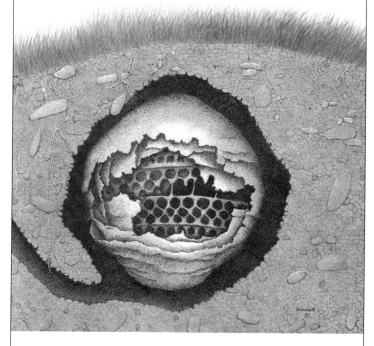

• The common wasp lives in colonies with as many as 20,000 members. For the most part, the workers construct the cells of the wasps' nest where the queen lays her eggs.
• Workers catch insects and feed them to the larvae.
• The wasps' nest is made of ground wood. This wood mixed with the wasp's saliva creates a material similar to paper pulp.
• Just before winter, the entire colony dies, except for a few young queens that have mated. After sleeping all winter, these queens will begin a new colony.
• There are several species of wasps. Most of them live in large, busy colonies but a few species live alone.

FOOD

- Wasps drink flower nectar the same way bees do. A wasp's tongue, however, is shorter than a bee's, so wasps visit only those flowers with nectar they can reach.
- In the summer, the workers may catch more than 4,000 flies and caterpillars each day. The victims are paralyzed by a worker's sting and brought to the wasps' nest as food for the larvae.

REPRODUCTION

- The queens that have hibernated come out of their sleep at the beginning of April. Each one begins to construct her nest, most often underground, but sometimes in a hole in a wall or under the eaves of a building. This construction is continued by the first workers that are born.
- The wasps' nest is made to hold a large number of cells. The queen lays an egg in each of them. When an egg hatches, a larva crawls out. It becomes an adult worker after about one month.
- At the end of the summer, new queens and males are born. The queens will mate with the males to create future populations of wasps.
- Wasp workers and males live for only one year. The cycle will begin again with a new queen.

THE WASP AND PEOPLE

- The wasp is feared for its painful sting. At the end of summer, wasps become bothersome. They search parks or picnic grounds for fruit and other sugary substances.
- It is only the workers that are capable of stinging. The stinger is composed of three parts. A long rigid tip called the stylet is at the very end.

Two jagged lancets are next to the sacks where the venom is stored. It is important to remember that the wasp does not deliberately attack people. It only stings to defend itself if it feels threatened. A wasp can pull its stinger out of a caterpillar, but the stinger gets stuck in a person's skin.

THREATS AND MEASURES OF CONSERVATION

- The wasp is a fearsome predator, eating a large number of flies and caterpillars. However, all around the world wasp populations are getting smaller. Why is this happening? One reason is that many people spray fruit and flowers with pesticides. Pesticides are toxic chemicals used to kill bugs. These pesticides are also deadly to wasps.
- Wasps help pollinate flowers and control bugs. We need to learn to see them as part of nature's plan.

THE LYNX

Perched on the roof of a 4-wheel drive truck, a zoologist adjusts an antenna. She exchanges a few words with her partner who is a biologist. The two scientists are worried. It has been nearly two weeks since they lost track of the lynx they had been following for months.

The scientists had caught the female lynx and fitted it with the special radio transmitting collar as part of a project to study lynx behavior during each season of the year. After releasing the lynx, the scientists tracked it using the radio signals from its collar to find out where it would go and how far it would travel each day.

What has happened to the lynx? Has she died, the victim of a poacher? Or has the radio transmitter broken?

"I'll try again at full power," says the zoologist. The minutes tick by. "There's something!" she exclaims. "I'm getting a weak signal." The signal is over 40 miles away, so the two pack their gear and quickly drive their truck in the direction of the signal. By nightfall, they know that the lynx is nearby in a quiet valley. The scientists decide to camp for the night.

The next day at dawn they begin their search again. At 5AM the rising sun casts soft rays of light on the rocks. Every 15 minutes the two scientists fine-tune their receiver. The radio signals are clear, but they are worried. According to their readings, the lynx is in the valley but has not moved since the day before. They fear she is caught in a trap or has eaten poisoned bait.

They scan the valley with their binoculars but see no movement for hours. Then, suddenly, as they climb across some rocks, they look up and see her. In one strong, graceful movement, the lynx steps forward onto a flat rock and lazily begins to wash herself. The scientists are overjoyed that she is safe. Suddenly, two small balls of fur appear behind the lynx. This is why the young female was not moving! She had come to the valley to give birth to her young!

LOCATION	DESCRIPTION	HABITAT	BEHAVIOR

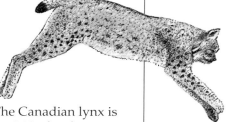

LOCATION

• The Canadian lynx lives in most of Canada as well as in Alaska, the northeastern, and the northwestern United States.
• Its cousin, the bay lynx or bobcat, lives in most of the United States and Mexico.
• The lynx of Europe, or the boreal lynx, at one time lived in all the forests of Europe. Today it is found only in Scandinavia.

DESCRIPTION

• The Canadian lynx is 32 to 36 inches long, not counting its tail, which measures 4 inches.
• The lynx weighs about 30 pounds.
• The fur of the lynx is reddish brown with dark brown spots in varying numbers, especially on its legs.
• The lynx has a very short tail which is completely black at the end. The bobcat's tail is black only at the very tip.
• Soft white tufts of hair grow out of its ears.
• The hind legs are much longer than the forelegs, which allows the animal to run very fast and to take great leaps.
• There are five toes on each front foot; four on each back foot. The claw on each toe can be retracted (pulled in).

HABITAT

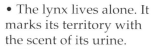

• The lynx lives in rocky or hilly terrain, in forested areas, and in swamps.

BEHAVIOR

• The lynx lives alone. It marks its territory with the scent of its urine.
• The lynx hunts during the night. In the winter, it may get hungry enough to hunt during the day.

• It can run very rapidly, but it does not usually chase its prey over long distances.
• Large feet help the lynx travel easily over deep snow.

FOOD

- Rabbits and snowshoe hares are the basis of its diet.
- The lynx may also eat a deer or a fawn, but it will only prey on the sick or weak.
- The lynx also eats mice, other small rodents, and birds.
- The population of rabbits and snowshoe hares goes up and down in an 8 to 10 year cycle. When this food source is low, lynx may attack domesticated animals.

The dropping of a wild animal is call its *spoor*.

REPRODUCTION

- The lynx mates at the end of winter, in February or March. Two to four young are born after two months.
- The mother makes a den underneath an uprooted tree, in a hollow log, or in another secret and hidden spot.
- The young are born with their eyes closed and are nursed for about three months. They remain with their mother until she mates again the following season.

THE LYNX AND PEOPLE

- For a very long time, the lynx was feared as a dangerous animal with cruel and bloodthirsty habits. People shot it to feel safe and to sell its fur. When a lynx attacked a farm animal, people felt justified in killing it.
- Not until after 1960 did people begin to study

and accept the lynx and its cousins, the bobcat and mountain lion. They all help to keep the rodent population in check, but stay as far away from people as possible. Now, the idea of protecting the lynx and helping the species multiply is accepted by many people.

THREATS AND MEASURES OF CONSERVATION

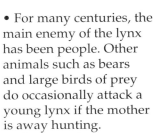

- For many centuries, the main enemy of the lynx has been people. Other animals such as bears and large birds of prey do occasionally attack a young lynx if the mother is away hunting.
- The lynx plays a positive role in controlling certain populations of rodents and hoofed animals. It will capture the older and weaker members of the group so that there is more food for the stronger members.
- Lynx hunting is against the law. The lynx population should continue to grow if the protective laws are enforced.

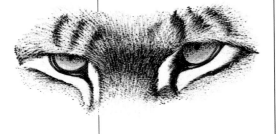

THE COMMON TOAD

In October, the toad ceased all activity. Sleeping under a tree stump, it spent winter in partial hibernation. Now it is March, and tonight, as the sun slowly sets on the horizon, the toad comes out of its hiding place. It is a male.

It moves at a regular pace, stretching its legs. One might think that it is going somewhere important, but when a beetle crosses its path, it stops. In a lightning-quick movement, the toad extends its long, sticky tongue, snaps up the insect, and immediately swallows it. Now the toad continues on its way. It is spring, and the instinct to reproduce irresistibly drives it. It will travel more than 50 yards, but the journey is definitely worth it to this determined batrachian (vertibrate amphibian).

However, the toad stops once again, as if frozen. Is it trying to decide which way to go? It hears rustling in the grass. A young hedgehog suddenly appears and moves toward the toad. The toad positions itself for defense. Head lowered and hindquarters upright, it swells itself up, filling its lungs. The young hedgehog is surprised. It sticks its little nose on the toad, then lightly nibbles at it. Ugh! What an awful smell and what a burning taste! The hedgehog retreats, sickened by the irritating liquid secreted from the skin of the toad.

Calm again, the toad resumes his march. Soon, he is no longer alone. Other toads approach the pond. The male sees a female and climbs onto her back.

At the pond, the numerous males actively fight over the few females. Toad love songs sound out. The melodious croaks are sometimes interrupted by a protesting ribbitt, when two foolish males collide. What a noisy night!

LOCATION	DESCRIPTION	HABITAT	BEHAVIOR	FOOD
• The common toad lives in North America and Europe.	• The common toad generally ranges in size from 3 1/2 to 5 1/2 inches. The females are larger than the males. • It has a heavy and thick body. • The head is large and flat, and the snout is quite short. • Toads are typically brown, but they vary in shades from olive green to a dark, reddish-brown. • Toads have very thick skin. On their backs, they have rough bumps called warts. • Special glands on their heads and necks produce a poison which helps keep predators from eating them. Most predators do not like the smell or taste of a toad. • The toad has large, bulging eyes with horizontal pupils.	• Common toads are not picky about where they live. The area can be dry or damp. Toads can be found in parks, swamps, forests, gardens, or even your own backyard. • They live on the plains as well as in the mountains. At the end of the winter, they move toward ponds and streams to mate.	• The common toad is active day and night. • It is able to move very quickly when necessary. It can leap, but less swiftly and not as high as the frog. It often remains motionless for a very long period of time. • At the end of each winter, toads faithfully return to their pond to reproduce. During mating season, toads may form a huge colony, but they are usually solitary animals. • In October, the toad retires to a safe hiding place in a stump or abandoned mouse tunnel. The toad then grows very sleepy and remains in a state of partial hibernation until mid-March of the following year. • Toads live a very long time. In the wild, they live from 7 to 10 years but can live up to 40 years in captivity.	• The toad eats ants and beetles as well as aphids, spiders, centipedes, caterpillars, worms, wood lice, fleas, and snails. Sometimes it eats wasps and bees. • It captures prey by shooting out its tongue which has a sticky tip.

REPRODUCTION

• In general, the males are the first to arrive at the body of water where mating will begin. After several days of mating, each female lays a series of blackish eggs in two long strings. The strings cling to vegetation in the pond. The tadpoles appear after only two weeks. During the next three months they will grow back, then front legs, lose their tails, develop air-breathing lungs, and become young toads.

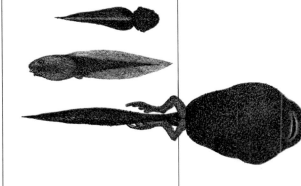

THE ENEMIES

• Many carnivorous animals do not eat the toad because of the smelly poison secreted by its skin. Other animals are not so choosy. Some snakes as well as the otter and the polecat will eat it. Crows will eat it too, but they are careful to skin it first.

THE TOAD AND PEOPLE

• Historically, the toad has filled people with dread. Some people thought that toads carried rabies in their saliva. Others thought that toads gave people warts. Myths once told that toads ate poisonous plants, and that in some rainstorms, toads fell out of the sky by the thousands.
• The toad's face and warty skin scare people.

It also frightens gardeners when it leaps up quickly and suddenly. During mating season, its nightly noise may sound creepy.
• The irritating liquid that the toad secretes is not dangerous to people. However, be careful not to touch your eyes if you have just picked up a toad. The secretions may cause your eyes to water.

THREATS AND MEASURES OF CONSERVATION

• Many toads get crushed as they cross busy highways and roads to reach mating areas.

SOLUTIONS

• Signs could warn drivers of an important toad crossing area.
• Barriers could be placed along the edge of roads to collect the toads so that they could be carried across safely.
• In some areas, barriers could channel the toads to tunnels passing beneath the roads.

THE VULTURE

In April, the snow in the Spanish mountains is glistening in the bright sunlight. A griffon vulture soars overhead using its wide, powerful wings to float on the rising warm air currents called thermals. Its beak is not strong enough to kill anything the way a hawk or an eagle can, so it is gliding along looking for animals that are already dead.

The vulture is very hungry. The expandable pouch, or crop, in its throat where it keeps extra food is empty. Traveling at about 40 miles an hour, its sharp eyes spot the body of a deer that has been killed on the road during the night. The vulture circles, still high in the sky, then it swoops down for a meal.

Out of nowhere, several other large brown birds appear and circle for a moment. Then they, too, dive down toward the carcass of the deer. With their feet shoved forward and their wings bent back, they land and hop toward the animal. One of them boldly hops right onto the deer. He spreads his wings slightly and leaps about, holding his talons in front of him. The other vultures back away a bit to give him room.

First he and then the others eat their fill, but now they are so full and heavy that they cannot take off. They must rest on the ground while they digest their meal.

LOCATION	DESCRIPTION	HABITAT	BEHAVIOR

• Vultures exist in North and South America, Europe, Africa, and Asia. The many families include the condors, turkey vultures, griffons, and king vultures.
• The family of griffon vultures range from Spain to Malaysia.

• Griffon vultures are brown with very short, white down covering the head and neck. (Most other vultures have no feathers on their head and neck.)
• The wings span up to 8 feet.
• In flight, the bird looks very large. The long primary feathers at the tips of its wings help it soar on air currents.

• The griffon vulture generally lives in rocky, mountainous areas or dry plateaus and other flat lands.

• Griffon vultures live in social groups and nest in colonies.
• The average vulture can fly for a very long time. It does not need to flap its wings as it soars on warm air currents.
• At times it likes to sunbathe, resting on a rock with its wings spread out.

• The vulture normally hunts alone. It seems to remain in contact with the other birds from the colony, however. When one vulture discovers a carcass, it flies in a circle to let the others know that it has found food. They do not call out to signal a find.

FOOD

• Vultures normally eat carrion, which means dead animals. Even though the animal may have died from disease, the vulture's strong digestive system destroys the germs.

REPRODUCTION

• Vultures begin to nest as early in the year as February. The female lays only one egg. The male and the female take turns sitting on the egg to keep it warm and to protect it. The incubation process lasts from 49 to 55 days.
• The young vulture eats what the parents bring back to the nest. The parents will regurgitate their food to feed their young. The young can begin to fly and seek its own food at the age of four months.

THE VULTURE AND PEOPLE

• In the past, the vulture was suspected of stealing sheep. Farmers and ranchers hunted vultures and tried to destroy them. Poisoned carcasses were placed out for the birds to eat.
• Today, we better understand the important role that this species plays in the ecosystem by getting rid of animal carcasses. The vulture helps to diminish the spread of disease and germs.
• People sometimes feel that vultures are ugly, dirty birds with disgusting habits, but vultures are beautiful in flight and are now seen as one of nature's ways to keep the Earth clean.

THREATS AND MEASURES OF CONSERVATION

• Vultures are protected in Europe and North America, but modern farming and ranching methods do not allow for much carrion.
• Pesticides harm the vultures and their eggs.

SOLUTIONS

• The vulture is now being reintroduced in areas where it was hunted before.
• Special captive breeding programs for the California condor have been effectively reintroducing it into the wild.
• Small vultures such as the black or turkey vultures have learned to coexist in harmony with people. If we let them satisfy their appetite for garbage, they can help us dispose of it.

THE WATER SNAKE

The river slowly meanders across the field. The landscape is almost motionless. Suddenly, there is a faint rustling sound in the reeds along the riverbank. A snake slithers into the water. It swims gracefully by waving its entire body from side to side and quickly moves toward the opposite bank. As the snake swims by, tiny fish flash up to the surface like chrome-plated darts. The snake normally eats small fish, but today it chases other, easier prey.

About ten tiny frogs hop onto the river bank just ahead of it. With unblinking eyes, the snake patiently watches the frogs. Its forked tongue slips in and out of its mouth like a flickering flame. This tongue serves as a sense of smell by picking up chemical sensations the way a nose does for other animals.

Now the snake slowly turns its head towards the nearest tiny frog. Like a spring that is suddenly released, the snake lunges with its mouth open, seizes the frog, and swallows it. Gulp!

The remaining small frogs leap away in all directions. Some jump into the water; others head for dry land away from the river bank. Calmly, the snake pursues the slower ones and methodically catches and eats them, too. About twenty young frogs disappear in this manner. What an appetite! Finally, the snake's hunger is satisfied. It slithers out of the water toward a clump of grass that the river waves have pushed back.

But now, a shadow moves across the riverbank. A heron lands abruptly on a nearby tree stump. It is a wading bird that eats frogs, fish, and whatever else it can catch. The snake realizes the danger, and very quickly disappears beneath the grass. Motionless, the heron watches and waits with its sword-sharp beak ready.

LOCATION

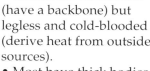

- Snakes are common on all continents except Antarctica. Water snakes are one of the most commonly feared types. Water snakes of the harmless Nerodia family may be 5 feet long.

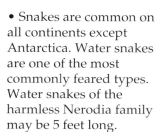

DESCRIPTION

- Snakes are vertebrates (have a backbone) but legless and cold-blooded (derive heat from outside sources).
- Most have thick bodies which they flatten when afraid.
- The coloration is variable from the Florida green water snake to the diamondback water snake of the Mississippi Valley. One of the most common types is the northern water snake, which has many different colors and markings.
- A snake's scale-covered body has no visible ear holes.

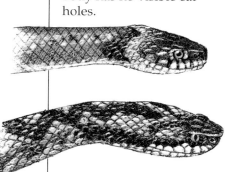

POISONOUS OR NOT?

- This is the first question to ask yourself when approaching a snake. Even though most are not poisonous, some will bite just because they feel threatened.

Harmless Water Snakes
- When alarmed, they hiss, flatten their bodies, or retreat into water, if possible.
- The head is the same width as the body.
- Its pupil is round.

Poisonous Snakes
- When alarmed, they vibrate their tails (cotton-mouth, rattlesnake, copperheads).
- The head of a poisonous snake is wider than the body and has a triangular shape.
- There is a deep pit on each side between the eye and nose. The pit is a sensory organ used to feel the warmth of prey.
- The pupil is vertical.

HABITAT

- Water snakes spend most of their lives in the water, hidden under rocks, logs, clumps of leaves, or in burrows. They may also be seen basking on a clump of grass, or on a log at the water's edge where they can slip silently into the water.

COLD-BLOODED REPTILES

- Warm-blooded birds and mammals produce heat internally. Reptiles depend on their environment for heat. When they are too warm, they may hide under rocks, earth, or wood. When they are too cold, they may slow down and go into a sort of hibernation.
- Reptiles search for their ideal temperature — about 75° to 85° F. An environment that is too hot or too cold can cause the death of the reptile.

FOOD

- Water snakes eat frogs, salamanders, fish, and crayfish found in or near the water.
- Poisonous water snakes also eat small birds and mice.

REPRODUCTION

- Most water snakes lay eggs which hatch immediately into miniature copies of their parents.
- Some young snakes have slightly different coloring than they will have as adults.
- Females lay eggs once a year, often in July, in a damp, warm place.

SNAKES AND PEOPLE

- By crawling on its belly, staring with a piercing look, and having fangs and poison to hunt and defend itself, the snake has been associated with the idea of evil, cruelty, and other negative qualities.
- Snakes are in the middle of the food chain. They eat large numbers of insects and rodents, and are themselves eaten by other predators. People are at the top of the food chain so we are dependent on all the rest, even if we do not eat snakes themselves.

THREATS AND MEASURES OF CONSERVATION

- People kill snakes because we cannot easily tell which ones are poisonous.
- Habitats that are suitable for snakes and other reptiles are being reduced as wetlands are drained and developed for roads and buildings.

Know your snakes

- If it has red, black, and yellow rings around its body, and the red and yellow are separated by black rings, it is probably a harmless milk snake or scarlet kingsnake.
- If the red and yellow rings are touching, it is probably a poisonous coral snake.
- Stay away from any snake with a tail ending in round segments. This is a rattlesnake or a water moccasin, both of which are poisonous.

THE WOLVES

It has been several days since the wolf pack has had a successful hunt. The leader of the pack trots along through the snow-covered forest with his fifteen followers close behind. As they search for food, they leave deep tracks in the snow that look like the foot prints of large dogs: a triangular area in the center with four oval toe prints around it. Four long gashes are the clear marks left by sharp claws.

Now, the leader stops and sniffs the ground. He turns and lets out several small yaps. He has picked up the scent of a herd of deer more than a mile away. The pack becomes very excited and alert. They set off at a gallop to get as close to their prey as possible without being seen by it.

The five wolf pups are old enough to keep up with the pack now. Six months old, they are nearly as big as their parents. The pups are learning how to hunt large prey which takes teamwork. Hunting alone, they can catch rabbits, mice, or other small animals, but to hunt deer, they must be cunning and use the combined strength of the pack to succeed.

Somehow, a few deer sense danger. They raise their heads and dart away briskly, rousing all of the herd to follow.

As the wolf pack chases the herd of deer, they separate from each other. The deer leap from side to side in panic. The wolf leader gives the signal for the attack. He charges at a deer that seems slower than the others. The pack circles the prey, trying to wear it out in a wild zigzag pursuit. After only a minute, the lead wolf manages to knock the deer off balance. The entire pack rushes in toward the victim. In a few instants, the hunt is over.

Teeth bared, the leader of the pack signals with a few menacing growls for the others to wait. After he eats, they may eat. When all have eaten, they begin the celebration with a chorus of howling.

Each wolf howl is a slightly different note. Together, they sound quite musical, but not to the people living on the ranch down in the valley.

Some of the people shudder at the thought of hungry wolves. They do not realize that the wolves are howling to celebrate their full stomachs and to affirm the bonds of family that help wolves to work together.

Howling before a hunt wouldn't make much sense. The deer would know exactly where the wolves were, and they would run away. The people, however, have heard too many stories about vicious wolves and are all too ready to be afraid.

LOCATION	DESCRIPTION	HABITAT	BEHAVIOR

• The wolf lives in North America and in parts of Europe.

• Wolves usually have brown fur, but it may be black, grey, or yellowish.
• The average male wolf is 5 to 6 1/2 feet long from its nose to the tip of its outstretched tail.
• The average wolf weighs 65 to 100 pounds. The leader of the pack is usually the biggest and strongest male. He may weigh 150 pounds.
• Like domestic dogs, wolves have 42 teeth including four larger canine teeth. In the wolf, however, the canine teeth may be 2 1/2 inches long.

• Wolves live in forests, by the edge of the woods, on flat lands, or in mountains. They also survive in open ranges, steppes, tundras, and taigas.
• Sometimes wolves will spend long periods of time in deep ravines or thick forests where it is difficult to track them.

• Wolves live in packs, but sometimes one will go off to live alone. The pack consists of an adult male and female and their young. A pack may have 7 to 15 members.
• The hunting of large prey depends on organized hunting behavior. Each wolf in the pack obeys complex rules of how to act during hunting, eating, playing, and living with its family.

• Like dogs, wolves show affection, loyalty, and intelligence in dealing with each other and sometimes with people.
• Wolves communicate with each other with sounds (yaps, growls, whines, and howls) and with body movements. For example, tail up, ears up, and fur fluffed are behaviors of dominance or content, while tail down, ears flat, and fur flat are behaviors of submission or fear.

FOOD

• The wolf hunts large prey such as caribou, moose, and deer. Smaller prey include hare, rabbit, and beaver. A very hungry wolf might also eat a small mouse or other rodent. Able to go without eating for up to two weeks, when the pack does make a kill, each animal might eat as much as twenty pounds of meat.

REPRODUCTION

• Mating is at the end of winter. The pups are born 60 to 63 days later. The litter may be from 2 to 10 pups. The average is 5.
• The female digs a den with her paws or uses a rock cave or hollow log as a den. The pack will supply her with food after the pups are born.
• Pups open their eyes in 5 to 9 days. They are nursed for 8 weeks and reach adult weight at 15 months.

THE WOLF AND PEOPLE

• People and wolves competed for food long ago when we lived by hunting. Native Americans respected the skill and strength of wolves. Some imitated wolves' hunting techniques.
• When people in Europe began to farm, about 1,200 years ago, they cut down the forests and found themselves surrounded by hungry wolves. It was very rare, however, that a wolf attacked a person. The only reason that a hungry wolf would even attack a farm animal is that farm animals seem like their normal prey. They are weak and cannot run fast enough to get away.
• Many fables and legends associate wolves with evil. The big bad wolf of fairy tales and the medieval tales of werewolves continue to influence people's attitudes towards wolves.

THREATS AND MEASURES OF CONSERVATION

• The wolf needs a lot of room in which to move around. As the human population grows, wolves are forced to withdraw onto wild and remote regions where prey is not easily found. In some regions, however, the wolf is a protected animal because human beings are beginning to realize what a splendid and interesting animal the wolf is.